Racism
and
Racial Resentment

Their Role In Trump's Election

∞∞∞∞∞

Black Lives Matter

∞∞∞∞∞

David King Keller, PhD

Racism

and

Racial Resentment
Their Role In Trump's Election

—

Black Lives Matter

—

David King Keller, PhD

© 2020 All rights reserved.

Printed in the United States of America.

Purchase or use of this book's contents in any manner is
acceptance of Publisher's Terms and Conditions.

Publisher: **Keller Research Institute,** 10950-60 San Jose
Blvd, Suite 100, Jacksonville, FL 32257. Email for Phone
number: DrDavidKingKeller@gmail.com

For media interviews or consulting:

send email with "Media" in subject line to:

DrDavidKingKeller@gmail.com

ISBN: 9798652618858

Table of Contents

Dedication 4

Preface 5

Racism and Racial Resentment 7

Exhibit 1 - Warriors Don't Cry 29

    A Best-Selling Book on Bravery In The Face of Racism By Dr. Melba Patillo Beals, One of the Little Rock Nine 29

Exhibit 2- Media Talking Points...............................30

About The Author 31

Publisher's Terms and Conditions............................38

Index..39

Dedication

George Floyd, Breonna Taylor, and Ahmaud Arbery

Preface

My father took me to a peaceful civil rights demonstration when I was in grade school. He was a West Point graduate, a career Army officer, and a leader in our church. He taught me fair play and that everyone deserved to be treated equally. He taught me to love my neighbor. He taught me that power should be used judiciously and practiced with an even hand. That is why much of what Donald Trump does is antithetical to what I believe.

Trump's appeal to racism attracts votes from millions who suffer from racial bigotry. This book is so well-documented that you will be able to see, hear, and feel the intensity of the racial prejudice that runs through the veins of millions of white Americans.

This book documents in detail, using studies and excerpts from published articles, how Donald Trump wins votes using racism. You will see the national poll where a majority of Americans call Trump a racist.

This book lists how many voters Trump can count on with his racist appeal. This book has studies that show millions who voted for Trump in 2016 were racists and voters experiencing racial resentment. You'll find out why the Republicans are called the "white grievance" party.

In this short book, Dr. Keller explores the impact of racism and racial resentment on Trump's 2016 election. That knowledge becomes a foundation to understand how Trump is already using a racist call-out strategy called a "dog-whistle" to bolster his support from racists, white nationalists, and those experiencing racial resentment and "white grievance" for his 2020 election.

You will learn about the enthusiasm poll and how Trump's commanding lead in that poll could help predict his 2020 victory. You will discover this and much, much more, so that you can fully understand *Racism and Racial Resentment, Their Role In Trump's Election.*

You will learn how fear and hate motivate voters to actually vote, a tactic that is more effective than nice platitudes. You will discover that a revved-up racist voter is a passionate voter, and passionate voters won't let pandemics stop them, while other less passionate voters are looking for excuses not to vote.

Whites who are uncomfortable with the growing minority becoming the new majority have what is called racial resentment. Trump knows how to play to that racial resentment feeling using racist dog whistles and his attacks on the new minority Congresswomen, called "The Squad."

Dr. Keller explains that even though this group of racial bigots are be in the minority, they show up to vote in a higher percentage than those less emotionally engaged in the Presidential election. That metric is called the "enthusiasm level" poll. This book shows how far ahead Trump is over Biden in that key poll and how it could decide the election.

Once you read this very short book, you'll be able analyze Trump's action within a more-informed context. It will explain why Trump took a uncompassionate "soul-less" law and order stance in response to the protests following the horrific death of George Floyd. On May 25, 2020, George Floyd, a 46-year-old black man, died in Minneapolis, Minnesota after a police officer knelt on his back and neck in a way that prevented his ability to breathe. Three other police officers stood nearby and watched. The video of this incident went viral and sparked more than a week of national protests. After reading this book's research, you will understand why Trump is abandoning the "average" American in favor of appealing to the millions of racists in his base as a deliberate political strategy.

Racism and Racial Resentment

Racists, white nationalists, and those experiencing racial resentment and white grievance all find a "friend" in Donald Trump.

In an election as tight as the 2016 election, every vote counted. The same holds true for 2020.

It is fairly common knowledge that racists feel comfortable with Trump. Let's review the data that proves it.

In general, you can say that racists preferred Donald Trump to Hillary Clinton in 2016, and the same will hold true for Trump vs. Biden in 2020.

"Trump Is Racist, Half of U.S. Voters Say" read the Quinnipiac Poll headline. A July 2019 Quinnipiac University national poll found that 51% say Trump is a racist; 45% say he is not.

When you peel back a layer of that 51% number who say Trump is a racist you find that only 9% who described themselves as Republican said Trump was a racist, while 86% of Democrats said Trump was a racist. 56% of those who self-identified as Independents said Trump was a racist.

In all age brackets above 18, the majority said Trump was a racist at an average rate of 52%.

Overall, by race, 46% of Whites said Trump was a racist, while Blacks were at 80%. White Evangelists were at 21%. Catholics at 46%. Those with no religious identification polled at 63% who said Trump was a racist.

The Quinnipiac report stated,

> "What this boils down to is that racism is detected, determined and observed through partisan and ideological lenses. This is hardly shocking. Yet what

is still quite striking is how much the perception of the importance of racism has changed in recent years. How else is it that the United States, a nation that declared 244 years ago that 'all men are created equal,' has a president seen as a racist by a majority of the electorate?"[1]

That many believe Trump is a racist was not news to many Trump supporters. Post-2016 election research, which we will review momentarily, has shown that Trump was supported by white national supremacists, other types of racists, and those experiencing "racial resentment" and "white grievance."

Thomas Edsall penned a 2020 New York Times op-ed titled, "How Racist Is Trump's Republican Party?"

Edsall has been teaching political journalism at Columbia University since 2006 and writes a weekly column from Washington, D.C. on politics, demographics, and inequality. In a March 18, 2020, New York Times op-ed Edsall states, "With Trump, the [Republican] Party has grown comfortable as a white grievance party. Is that racist? Yes, I think it is. [Nearly 63 million people voted for Trump in 2016.] Are 63 million-plus people who supported Trump racist? No, absolutely not. But to support Trump is to make peace with white grievance and hate."

Edsall refers to Stuart Stevens, who "has impeccable Republican credentials," a lead strategist for George W.

---

1. Staff, "Trump Is Racist, Half of U.S. Voters Say, Quinnipiac University National Poll Finds," *Quinnipiac University*, July 30, 2019, https://poll.qu.edu/national/release-detail?ReleaseID=3636

Bush, and clients that have included Mitt Romney and other current and former senators. In his new book, *It Was All A Lie*, Stevens writes, "I can't keep lying to myself to ward off the depressing reality that I had been lying to myself for decades. There is nothing strange or unexpected about Donald Trump. He is the logical conclusion of what the Republican Party became over the last fifty or so years, a natural product of the seeds of race, self-deception, and anger that became the essence of the Republican Party. Trump isn't an aberration of the Republican Party; he is the Republican Party in a purified form.

Stevens goes on to say, "I have no one to blame but myself," he declares on the first page. "What I missed was one simple reality: it was all a lie." Edsall explains, "What were the lies? That the Republican Party 'espoused a core set of values: character counts, personal responsibility, strong on Russia, the national debt actually mattered, immigration made America great, a big-tent party.'" And what, to Stevens, is the truth? The Republican Party is "just a white grievance party."

Edsall states,
> "In fact, Stevens told me, 'race is the original sin of the modern Republican Party…' Stevens's comment demonstrates the difficulty many analysts have pinning down the meaning of racism and the distinction — if there is one — between being a racist and voting for a racist."

Edsall asks the question, "Is the modern Republican Party built on race prejudice, otherwise known as racism?"[2]

----

2. Thomas B. Edsall, "How Racist Is Trump's Republican Party?" *New York Times,* March 18, 2020,

As we contemplate that question let's gain an appreciation for a feeling gripping many Americans, racial resentment.

A vox.com article on December 15, 2017, by German Lopez, in referring to the 2016 presidential election, was titled, *The past year of research has made it very clear: Trump won because of racial resentment.*[3]

Lopez refers to four studies. Here he speaks about one of them,

> More than a year after President Donald Trump won the election, there are still some questions about what drove him to victory: Was it genuine anxiety about the state of the economy? Or was it racism and racial resentment?
>
> Over at the Washington Post, researchers Matthew Fowler, Vladimir Medenica, and Cathy Cohen have published the results of a new survey on these questions, with a focus on the 41 percent of white millennials who voted for Trump and the sense of "white vulnerability" that motivated them. The conclusion is very clear:
>
> Contrary to what some have suggested, white millennial Trump voters were not in more economically precarious situations than non-Trump voters. Fully 86 percent of them reported being employed, a rate similar to non-Trump voters, and they were 14 percent less likely to be low income

https://www.nytimes.com/2020/03/18/opinion/trump-republicans-racism.html

3. German Lopez, "The past year of research has made it very clear: Trump won because of racial resentment," *Vox*, Dec 15, 2017, https://www.vox.com/identities/2017/12/15/16781222/trump-racism-economic-anxiety-study

than white voters who did not support Trump. Employment and income were not significantly related to that sense of white vulnerability. So, what was? Racial resentment."

How do we measure the impact of those millennials referred to in the study? Here are the numbers:

Pew Research defines a 2016 millennial as someone 20-35 years of age.[4]

Wikipedia tells us:

By analyzing U.S. Census data they found that in 2016 there were an estimated 71 million millennials, based on Pew's definition of the generation which ranges from 1981 to 1996, compared to 74.1 million Baby Boomers. Millennial population size varies, depending on the definition used.[5]

According to CNN Business, there are 76 million baby boomers, and 72% of them are white. The millennials are an even larger group with 87 million, but much more diverse — only 56% are white. https://cnn.it/3fEe51Y

Using the research cited above there are 87m millennials times 56% who are white equals 48.7m white millennials. We know from above that 41% of white millennials voted for Trump. 41% times 48.7 million equals 20 million millennials voted for Trump according to the Washington Post (WAPO) study that said racial resentment was a primary motivating factor for them.

---

4. Michael Dimock, "Defining generations: Where Millennials end and Generation Z begins," *Pew Research,* January 17, 2019, https://www.pewresearch.org/fact-tank/2019/01/17/where-millennials-end-and-generation-z-begins/

5. Wikipedia, "Millennials," Wikipedia, March 12, 2020, https://en.wikipedia.org/wiki/Millennials

With Trump receiving a total vote of 62.9 million, then, according to the Washington Post study, Trump's millennials accounted for about 31.7% of his vote. And according to the Washington Post article, their primary motivating factor was racial resentment. Millennials in that 2017 study were 18 to 34 years old. So, when you add in people, other than millennials, who are racist or have racial resentment or white grievance and voted for Trump, you have a number much higher than 31.7% or 20 million.

The WAPO research added this: "The survey looked at millennials because they would be the largest share of the voting-eligible population in 2018, so they're an important bellwether for future trends." (At the same time, most millennials backed Hillary Clinton in 2016, not Trump.)

To anyone who's been following the research on this, the findings should come as little surprise. There have now been numerous studies that found support for Trump is closely linked to racial resentment, defined by Fowler, Medenica, and Cohen as "a moral feeling that blacks violate such traditional American values as individualism and self-reliance."

Understanding this research is crucial to understanding Trump's rise. As a presidential candidate, Trump made a wide range of racist comments. Examples include suggesting that Mexican immigrants are criminals and rapists, proposing a ban on all Muslims entering the US, saying a U.S. judge should recuse himself from a case simply because of his Mexican heritage, and deploying dog whistles about "law and order."

As President, Trump equated a group of neo-Nazis, white supremacists, and white nationalists who descended onto Charlottesville, Virginia, with the anti-racism protesters who stood against bigotry.

The studies suggest that these kinds of comments and actions are not just incidental to Trump; they are at the core of his political success. If Democrats want to defeat Trump, they will need to find a way to overcome that racial resentment.

This is not a one-off finding. At this point, the evidence that a significant reason for Trump's rise was driven by racism and racial resentment is well established.

One paper, published in January by political scientists Brian Schaffner, Matthew MacWilliams, and Tatishe Nteta, found that voters' measures of sexism and racism correlated much more closely with support for Trump than economic dissatisfaction after controlling for factors like partisanship and political ideology.[6]

Another study, conducted by researchers Brenda Major, Alison Blodorn, and Gregory Major Blascovich, found that "if people who strongly identified as white were told that nonwhite groups will outnumber white people in 2042, they became more likely to support Trump."[7]

Lopez speaks for many writers and researchers when he states,

> "The evidence suggests, in fact, that the best way to weaken people's racial or other biases is through frank, empathetic dialogue. Given that, the strongest approach to really combating racism and racial resentment may be empathy." Not agreement,

---

6. German Lopez, "Study: racism and sexism predict support for Trump much more than economic dissatisfaction," *Vox*, Jan 4, 2017, https://www.vox.com/identities/2017/1/4/14160956/trump-racism-sexism-economy-study

7. German Lopez, "Half of Republicans say increased racial diversity will be "mostly negative"," *Vox*, July 24, 2018, https://www.vox.com/policy-and-politics/2018/7/24/17607608/racial-diversity-republicans-democrats

empathy. "I hear you." "I feel the concerns you're sharing." "I see what you're describing." Sticking with the same visual, auditory, or kinesthetic predicate genre that the other party is using is very important when seeking to establish rapport in order to create an opening for change.

The above research explains why Trump will periodically make racially charged statements and "dog whistles." Why? Because, by doing that, he is speaking directly to a very large segment of his base.

Shawn McElwee and Jason McDaniel wrote a May 8, 2017, article in TheNation.com titled *Economic Anxiety Didn't Make People Vote Trump, Racism Did*. They came to the same conclusion as cited in the above-referenced studies: racial resentment and racism were a large reason for Trump's victory.[8]

Here are the titles and reference sources for four studies that demonstrate that racism and racial resentment motivated many to vote for Trump: "Why 41 percent of white millennials voted for Trump,"[9] "Understanding White Polarization in the 2016 Vote for President: The Sobering

---

8. Sean McElwee & Jason McDaniel, "Economic Anxiety Didn't Make People Vote Trump, Racism Did," *The Nation,* May 8, 2017, https://www.thenation.com/article/archive/economic-anxiety-didnt-make-people-vote-trump-racism-did/

9. Matthew Fowler, Vladimir E. Medenica and Cathy J. Cohen, "Why 41 percent of white millennials voted for Trump," *Washington Post,* December 15, 2017, https://www.washingtonpost.com/news/monkey-cage/wp/2017/12/15/racial-resentment-is-why-41-percent-of-white-millennials-voted-for-trump-in-2016/

Role of Racism and Sexism,"[10] "The threat of increasing diversity: Why many White Americans support Trump in the 2016 presidential election,"[11] and "Supporters and opponents of Donald Trump respond differently to racial cues: An experimental analysis."[12]

The above studies explain Trump's very public Tweet attack on four minority newly-elected women in Congress as being Un-American on July 14, 2019, and his doubling down on these attacks while visiting a "Made In America" exhibit on July 15, 2019. A large group within Trump's base loves those attacks. This group and many other Americans are feeling very uncomfortable with the new America increasingly catering to, and run by, minorities.

For many Americans, their resentment toward minorities is increased when new minority Americans increasingly don't feel that it is necessary that they adapt to American language and customs. Basically, it's true, many Americans who would never define themselves as racist are experiencing a

---

10. Brian F. Schaffner, Matthew MacWilliams, and Tatishe Nteta, "Understanding White Polarization in the 2016 Vote for President: The Sobering Role of Racism and Sexism," *Political Science Quarterly*, March 25, 2018, https://doi.org/10.1002/polq.12737, https://onlinelibrary.wiley.com/doi/full/10.1002/polq.12737

11. Brenda Major, Alison Blodorn, Gregory Major Blascovich, "The threat of increasing diversity: Why many White Americans support Trump in the 2016 presidential election," *Sage Journals*, October 20, 2016,
https://journals.sagepub.com/doi/full/10.1177/1368430216677304, https://doi.org/10.1177/1368430216677304

12. Matthew D. Luttig, Christopher M. Federico, and Howard Lavine, "Supporters and opponents of Donald Trump respond differently to racial cues: An experimental analysis," *Sage Journals*, November 1, 2017, https://doi.org/10.1177/2053168017737411

feeling that the country they grew up loving is disappearing and transforming too quickly for them to feel comfortable with, and adjust to, the changes. That creates a type of racial uncomfortableness that researchers are calling racial resentment.

How many racists and white nationalists are there? A lot.

Enough to make a difference in a tight election? Yes.

Remember George Bush won the U.S. Presidential election by only 537 votes. That was the margin that gave Bush the State of Florida in the contested recount when the U.S. Supreme Court intervened and ordered the recount to stop, leaving Bush with a victory in Florida and with Florida's 29 Electoral College votes, the Presidency.

This does not mean racists elected Bush, but you'll read in "Reason #20" on Voter Suppression in my book titled, *Why Trump Won The 2020 Election, 21 Reasons Democrats Lost*, that a lawsuit and research proved that over 3,000 African-Americans in Florida who wanted to vote for Gore were prevented from doing so.

So, yes, racists and nationalists could determine the winner in a squeaky tight election, which is a good description of the 2020 race.

Racist support for Trump was highlighted during the 2016 election by Democratic contender Hillary Clinton.

It was August during the 2016 election cycle, and Hillary Clinton gave a speech[13] dedicated to denouncing the "alt-right"—a loosely associated set of white people who love Trump and embrace white-nationalist views that are too

---

13. Grace Wyler, "How Hillary Clinton's Attack on the Alt-Right Went Wrong," *Vice*, Aug 27, 2017, https://www.vice.com/en_us/article/5gqgvq/what-hillary-clinton-missed-in-her-alt-right-speech

extreme for most "regular" Republicans. Then, during one Friday speech, Clinton went further, saying that half of her opponent's supporters should be in a "basket of deplorables." She went on: "The racist, sexist, homophobic, xenophobic, Islamophobic—you name it. And unfortunately, there are people like that. And he has lifted them up."

Trump responded by denouncing Clinton's "low opinion" of Americans, and Clinton did apologize[14] for saying "half," though she stood behind most of the substance of her speech.

Was Clinton right? Were half of Trump's 2016 supporters' racists?

Jason McDaniel, a political scientist at San Francisco State University, was asked that question in September 2016 by Allie Conti of Vice.com. McDaniel explained the results of a recent study he conducted about the correlation of what people in the field call "racial resentment" and support for Donald Trump, and he told Allie that Clinton's original comments weren't far off.[15]

So, yes, political research based on 25 years of profiling by McDaniel's research group of U.S. voters indicated that <u>half the people voting for Trump in 2016 were racists</u>, or experiencing "racial resentment."

---

14. Seema Mehta, "Clinton apologizes for calling half of Trump's supporters 'deplorables'," *Los Angeles Times*, September 10, 2016, https://www.latimes.com/politics/la-na-pol-clinton-deplorables-20160910-snap-story.html

[15]. Sean McElwee & Jason McDaniel, "Economic Anxiety Didn't Make People Vote Trump, Racism Did," *The Nation*, May 8, 2017, https://www.thenation.com/article/archive/economic-anxiety-didnt-make-people-vote-trump-racism-did/

To fight racism against the south of the border immigrants, Democrats and those immigrants need a charismatic champion. They need a respected leader and orator like Dr. Martin Luther King who comes out of the south of the border migrant population. Caesar Chavez fought and won for the southern immigrant farmworkers. Now pro-immigrant supporters need an even bigger visionary to represent the best and brightest of all the southern border immigrants. Who is the current voice of the southern border immigrant? Does anyone come to mind? We have some names in Congress who are speaking out, Kamala Harris, Alexandria Ocasio-Cortez, Bernie Sanders and Elizabeth Warren, but they do not come from the maligned group.

The nationalists, racists, and people that feel extremely uncomfortable with the growth of minorities in America make up a sizeable single-issue voting bloc. People who fear the dilution of the "great American." Are these new immigrants coming across the southern border going to improve these types of contributions or dilute America's ability to come up with the next great invention? Research cited in this book indicates that it's these questions and others, at a nearly unconscious feeling level that helps to feed the anti-non-European immigrant feelings. Those folks might experience a slight attitude adjustment with a brief visit to this article titled, "5 self-made Hispanic immigrant millionaires."[16]We know about great immigrants from Europe, but do you know about these great Americans from Tijuana, Guadalajara, El Salvador, Columbia, and Argentina? Alberto "Beto" Perez is the founder of Zumba. Maria Contreras-Sweet is the former administrator of the SBA and founder of ProAmérica Bank. Jordi Munoz is the

----

16. Chris Morris, "5 self-made Hispanic immigrant millionaires," *CNBC*, June 12, 2017, https://www.cnbc.com/2017/06/12/5-self-made-hispanic-us-immigrant-millionaires.html

founder of 3D Robotics. Carlos Castro is president and CEO of Todos Supermarket. Jorge Pérez, co-founder and CEO of The Related Group. Like Trump, Perez made his fortune in real estate. As reported by CNBC,

> "Born in Argentina, Jorge Pérez came to the United States in 1968 after finishing high school. Settling in Miami, he, perhaps more than anyone else, is responsible for the skyline of that city. Pérez has a net worth of $2.8 billion, according to Forbes, and has been called "The condo king of South Florida" by the Wall Street Journal.

South of the border immigrants need a charismatic orator-representative who shows us how great many of these southern border immigrants are, what a great contribution they are making now, and can make in the future. The "sense" of what it means to be a Caucasian American as the non-white immigrants start to become the new majority has to change from what, for many, is an extremely uncomfortable, even aggravating experience to one of hope and excitement about sharing in this new cultural shift. Easier said than done.

Brookings reports that the "U.S. will become minority-white by 2045." They also report that for certain age groups of whites will become the minority much sooner. "Census projections indicate that for youth under 18–the post-millennial population–minorities will outnumber whites in 2020. For those age 18-29–members of the younger labor force and voting age populations–the tipping point will occur in 2027."[17]

---

17. William H. Frey, "The US will become 'minority white' in 2045, Census projects," *Brookings.edu*, March 14, 2018, https://www.brookings.edu/blog/the-avenue/2018/03/14/the-us-will-become-minority-white-in-2045-census-projects/

This sense of positional loss by Caucasians, of becoming the new minority, can cause them to lean toward a man like Trump because he wants to harken back to a time when whites were in the vast majority, and there was no such thing as "press 2" for Spanish. How long will it be before it's "press 2 for English"? How long before our Congress looks like the U.N with multiple languages spoken on Capitol Hill and laws are passed in multiple languages? These are their fears. This is a difficult future for the average white person to consider. It's an identity-level loss. Ask any psychologist, a person's self-identity lies at the heart of who they think they are and how they perceive themselves and their place in the world. An affront to one's identity strikes at deep psychic nerves that can trigger strong emotional responses. A diminishment of one's national cultural identity can easily form the basis for "racial resentment." Trump plays to that sentiment and therefore attracts people having this experience.

Twenty-five years of research went into political scientist Jason McDaniel's testing the study's "racial resentment" questions. McDaniel's study asks these "racial resentment indicator" questions on every one of his major national-election surveys. When Trump supporters' racial resentment numbers are compared to past Candidates and Presidents, the Trump supporters "were off the scale."

Racial resentment was not previously a significant dividing characteristic between the two major parties. Now, it's pretty clear that one of the major factors that split Democrats and Republicans is their views on racial resentment. If white people are more racially sympathetic, generally, they're going to be Democrats. If they're more racially "conservative" or resentful white people, they're likely going to feel more comfortable with the Republican Party. McDaniel said,

> I don't think that more people hold explicitly racist views, but it's more likely that those messages are getting out and being amplified by politicians. I think we are seeing an emergence of something that's scary and that we should be worried about.

What some think may be the "ultimate racist act" by Trump is still in progress.

The "ultimate racist act" by the Republican Party may be the ongoing attempt to eliminate the primary claim to fame by the Country's first black President, the Affordable Care Act (ACA). These Republicans had nothing to replace the Affordable Care Act, but all they knew was that the ACA had to go, regardless of the fact that doing so would take away the health care of 30 million Americans. Many ask, "How racist are you that you want to insult a black President so badly that you're willing to throw 30 million Americans under the bus?"

Others say there was another reason Republicans wanted to eliminate ACA. In a Washington Post article, Matt Obrien penned an article titled, "Why do Republicans want to repeal Obamacare so much? Because it would be a big tax cut for the rich." Maybe it wasn't racism, but personal wealth enhancement. Others say, "look at everything Trump does through the filter of trying to diminish a black President." Trump fired the White House Pandemic staff set up by Obama. Why would he do that? Trump refused to use the Pandemic Playbook created under black-President Obama. Why would he do that? In a national crisis where Americans are suffering and dying, a compassionate and caring leader turns to every resource available. That is unless, of course, you're Trump, and that the above theory is correct. Then, Trump wasn't going to turn to a national crisis solution created by a black man, regardless of the cost in American lives. Because who, then, if the Obama-sourced pandemic playbook worked, would be the hero? The black man who had the foresight or a President who used the black man's game book? It's just a theory some have, but then, there is this next headline.

On August 15, 2019, *Wired* ran this headline, "The Trump Admin Is Scrubbing Obamacare From Government Sites." The article stated, "According to a new report, the Trump administration has been systematically wiping crucial information about the ACA from government websites over the past two years."[18] ACA is, for now, the law of the land. Why would you deliberately make access to the program harder for Americans who need it?

While we think about that question, we must acknowledge the primary objection by many to the ACA was the required federally "mandated" penalty fee if you did not have proof of health insurance. That fee was put in place to help offset the federal government's cost to cover uninsured people. That federally mandated fee was eliminated in 2019. Others objected to the new ACA tax on investment income earnings above $200,000. Another objection to the ACA was, "we don't want the government getting involved in our healthcare." That objection fell on deaf ears for most because Medicare, a government healthcare program, has been around since 1965 and is extremely popular and deemed very successful by nearly every measurement.

The goal of these so-called "Republi**kkk**ans" (a spelling used often on the Internet) from Day 1 of the Obama

---

18. Issie Lapowsky, "The Trump Admin Is Scrubbing Obamacare From Government Sites," *Wired*, May 15, 2019, https://www.wired.com/story/trump-scrubbing-obamacare-from-government-sites/

administration was, apparently, to make sure Obama had no positive legacy. So, when they could, they blocked every attempt at legislation no matter how beneficial to the average American. Helping Americans was not as important as it was to prevent an African-American Obama from having any claims to fame as President. Some say the ongoing attempt to strip the ACA, also known as Obamacare, from Obama's legacy regardless of the cost to 30 million American human lives, is the ultimate racist act.

Many feel that Trump is pandering to racists and racial resentment when he criticizes "The Squad," four new 2018 Congresswomen, who come from minority backgrounds.

On July 14, 2019, these four freshmen minority congresswomen were the apparent targets of a Twitter rant by Trump. "Why don't they go back and help fix the totally broken and crime-infested places from which they came. Then come back and show us how it is done," he tweeted.

Four new Congresswomen have collectively come to be known as "The Squad." They are Reps. Alexandria Ocasio-Cortez, D-N.Y. (Puerto Rican on her mother's side), Ilhan Omar, D-Minn. (born in Somalia), Ayanna Pressley, D-Mass. (African-American); and Rashida Tlaib, D-Mich. (born in Detroit to Palestinian immigrant parents).

Trump sparked outrage by appearing to tell the four congresswomen – three of whom were born in the U.S. – to "go back" and fix the countries "from which they came" before trying to make changes in the U.S. The national newspaper USA Today on July 15, 2019 quoted people as saying, "This is what racism looks like."

When Trump attacks "The Squad," many of the racists, and those with racial resentment, in the Trump camp light up with joy.

Racists, white nationalists, those experiencing racial resentment, and racial discontent, also called "white grievance," are a very reliable niche of Trump voters.

The research discussed above shows that 20 million millennials who voted for Trump were experiencing racial resentment.[19] Other research that about half, or more, of all Trump supporters, were experiencing racial resentment and racial discontent, also called "white grievance."[20]

Another act by Trump that some will consider laced with racism was described in this headline in the Atlanta Journal-

---

19. Matthew Fowler, Vladimir E. Medenica and Cathy J. Cohen, "Why 41 percent of white millennials voted for Trump," *Washington Post*, December 15, 2017, https://www.washingtonpost.com/news/monkey-cage/wp/2017/12/15/racial-resentment-is-why-41-percent-of-white-millennials-voted-for-trump-in-2016/

20. Sean McElwee & Jason McDaniel, "Economic Anxiety Didn't Make People Vote Trump, Racism Did," *The Nation,* May 8, 2017, https://www.thenation.com/article/archive/economic-anxiety-didnt-make-people-vote-trump-racism-did/

Constitution, "Trump won't hang Obama portrait in White House."

On May 20, 2020, the *Atlanta Journal-Constitution* reported, "With public contention bubbling between President Donald Trump and former President Barack Obama, sources close to the president say Trump will break a 40-year tradition by refusing to unveil Obama's portrait at White House."[21] Racism or politics, or both?

As detailed above, statistical research proves that racists, nationalists, and whites who are experiencing racial resentment and "white grievance" were predominantly Trump supporters. This was one reason, the Democrats lost millions of votes in the 2016 election and will, again, lose millions of votes to Trump in the 2020 election.

Finally, remember that racists who support Trump seem to be more enthusiastic about voting for their candidate than those who are not racists and prefer Biden.

It's called the "strong enthusiasm" poll. Let's look at that poll in 2016.

The "likely voter" preference level for Clinton dropped below Trump's in the last week of the campaign. In fact, according to the *ABC News/Washington Post* poll support for Clinton was 12 points above Trump on October 23, 2016, 50% to 38%; but by October 30, 2016, Clinton went down 5 points, and Trump went up 8 points in just one week to 46% in favor of Trump to Clinton's 45%. That same poll also

---

21. Stephanie Toone, "Trump won't hang Obama portrait in White House," Atlanta Journal-Constitution," May 20, 2020, https://www.ajc.com/news/report-trump-will-break-year-tradition-refusing-unveil-obama-portrait-white-house/LAwFzNRII8zTCX9WLVKP0N/

measured "strong enthusiasm." In that enthusiasm poll, Clinton was significantly behind Trump on October 30th (8 days before the election), Trump was 53% to Clinton's 45%, for a strong enthusiasm gap of 8%. That is a huge gap. People will look for reasons not to vote, and in a close race, the enthusiasm gap can predict a winner.[22]

There are two key takeaways from the above information. One, Electoral College math decides everything. So, do what Trump did. Let go of the states you cannot possibly win and focus on those states that can swing either way called the battleground or "swing" states. Two, enthusiasm level is next in importance if voter preference of "likely voters" is close.

In Spring of 2020, Joe Biden had a large debilitating "strong enthusiasm" gap when compared to Trump. This is critical.

A March 29, 2020, *ABC/ Washington Post* enthusiasm poll had Biden trailing Trump by 29 percentage points in the high-level enthusiasm segment.[23]

That is a bone-crushing difference and bodes ill for Biden, if he cannot close that gap before November 3, 2020.

It's believed by this researcher that Trump's racist supporters will not let a little thing like a Fall resurgence of the pandemic keep them from voting. But it may slow down less enthusiastic supporters for Biden.

---

22. ABC News/Washington Post poll, "Strong Enthusiasm Ebbs for Clinton; Trump is +1 in Vote," *Langerresearch.com*, November 1, 2016, https://www.langerresearch.com/wp-content/uploads/1184a102016ElectionTrackingNo10.pdf

23. Sofi Sinozich, "Biden consolidates support, but trails badly in enthusiasm: Poll," *ABC News,* March 29, 2020, https://abcnews.go.com/Politics/biden-consolidates-support-trails-badly-enthusiasm-poll/story?id=69812092

In my other two books on the 2020 election, I discuss the fact that the national popularity poll in a close race is not as indicative of who will win the 2020 election as four other polls.

I identify those four other polls in my two companion books on the 2020 election titled, *Why Trump Won The 2020 Election, 21 Reasons Democrats Lost,* and *How Democrats Win The 2020 Election, 12 Steps To Victory*. That first book is a well-documented "tough love" wake-up call to the Democratic Party. That book has nearly 400 footnotes. It's also highly educational as to the impact of the Electoral College, third parties, and Independent voters.

How Democrats Win The 2020 Election, 12 Steps To Victory describes what the Democrats must do to beat Trump. The book first reviews messaging errors by the Democrats and the 26 alleged federal crimes committed by Donald Trump. The criminal allegations against Trump include full citations as to the criminal code statutes and a clear presentation of the publicly available evidence.

In conclusion, remember, racists vote because their racism is born of passion, usually fear and hate. Fear and hate are big motivators. People may "like" Biden, but will they vote for him? Will Biden supporters face down a resurging pandemic? Will Biden voters stand in long voting lines caused by Trump's 50,000 precinct voter challengers?

Yes, there is a Republican program that envisions recruiting up to 50,000 volunteers in 15 key states to monitor polling places and challenge ballots and voters deemed suspicious. That is part of a $20 million plan that also allots millions to challenge lawsuits by Democrats and voting-rights advocates seeking to loosen state restrictions on balloting, such as allowing vote by mail.[24]

The stakes are high. Trump will target predominantly black precincts with his 50,000 recruits to discourage voters in an effort at black voter suppression. It will take a great deal of passion and fortitude to overcome this wave of hostile activity designed to keep blacks from voting.

On the other hand, passionate racists will show up to vote for Trump no matter what. Will the Biden opposition show up with equal enthusiasm? If you are reading this after November 4, 2020, you know the answer.

God bless America. Please.

---

[24]. Charles P. Pierce, "Republicans Have Turned to Full-On Voter Intimidation in 2020," *Esquire*, May 18, 2020, https://www.esquire.com/news-politics/politics/a32583391/republicans-voter-intimidation-2020/

Exhibit 1 - Warriors Don't Cry

**A Best-Selling Book on Bravery In The Face of Racism
By Dr. Melba Patillo Beals, One of the Little Rock Nine**

Other must-read books by Dr. Melba Patillo Beals:

Beals, Melba Pattillo. *Warriors Don't Cry: A Searing Memoir of the Battle to Integrate Little Rock's Central High*. New York: Pocket Books, 1994. ISBN 0-671-86638-9

Beals, Melba Pattillo. *White Is a State of Mind: A Memoir*. Putnam Adult, 1999. ISBN 0-399-14464-1

Beals, Melba Pattillo. *March Forward, Girl: From Young Warrior to Little Rock Nine*. HMH Books for Young Readers, 2018. ISBN 1328882128

Beals, Melba Pattillo. *I Will Not Fear: My Story of a Lifetime of Building Faith under Fire*. Revell, 2018. ISBN 0800729439

Exhibit 2- Media Talking Points

- Multiple studies show impact of racism and racial resentment in 2016 election. Same for 2020 election?

- Trump Administration is scrubbing Obamacare from government sites making it more difficult for people to understand and use this US Government program. Is that racist?

- Trump breaks tradition and refuses to hang Obama portrait in the White House. Racism or politics?

- Three studies explain the political "strategy" behind Trump's attack on four freshman Congresswomen, "the Squad," telling them to go back from where they came. A racist dog-whistle?

- What is the "enthusiasm poll" and what role did it play in Trump's 2026 election, and what role will it play in the 2020 election?

- What are Dr. Keller's civil rights experiences?

- Is voter suppression of African-American votes racism or just an attempt to stifle Democratic voters? Both?

About The Author

David King Keller, PhD is a best-selling legal author, political analyst, and communication strategist.

Below are Dr. Keller's identification cards when he was working with Dr. Martin Luther King's Poor People's Campaign, which was affiliated with the Southern Christian Leadership Conference, SCLC.

Dr. Keller was Chairman of the Dr. Martin Luther King's Poor People's Campaign Support Committee at the University of Maryland, where he trained as a nurse's assistant to help the residents of Resurrection City.

Resurrection City was a series of tents set up on the Washington DC mall to act as a lobbying group to bring attention to the plight of the poor in America. Dr. Keller wanted to assist with the medical care of the residents but was, instead, asked to be a "Peace Brother" and help with perimeter security dealing with all the curious onlookers, tourists, and others. At the time, Dr. Keller was a pre-law major at the University of Maryland at College Park just outside of Washington, DC. He received a very well-paying summer job learning Federal law practices at the US Federal Marshal's Office just blocks from the Capitol. After only two days on the job, when Dr. Keller was told that the office was going to be involved in removing the residents of Resurrection City, he immediately quit. He then became the International Co-Director of Operation Outrage, which is discussed below.

The photo below of Dr. Keller's Martin Luther King's Poor People's Campaign IDs have greater clarity in color, but reproducing them in color would force Amazon to double the price of this book.

Dr. Melba Patillo Beals, one of the Little Rock Nine, is a civil rights hero who has experienced harrowing near-death experiences from racists. Dr. Beals' book, *Warriors Don't Cry*, is a gut-wrenching international best-seller, and a must-read as a primer on the foundation of racism in America. Dr. Keller had the honor of meeting nine American civil rights heroes, the Little Rock Nine. The Little Rock Nine endured unspeakable acts of racism when they integrated the all-white Little Rock High School following Brown v Board of Education.

In 1999, as a guest of Dr. Melba Patillo Beals, Dr. Keller had the honor of meeting all the civil rights heroes of the Little Rock Nine at a White House event. In a ceremony where President Bill Clinton quoted from Dr. Beals' book, *Warriors Don't Cry*, Dr. Beals, along with the other members of the famous Little Rock Nine, received the Congressional Gold Medal, the Nation's highest civilian honor. The White House ceremony honored the suffering, abuse, and life-endangering sacrifices that they all endured as leaders in the American civil rights movement. They all suffered from unspeakable acts of racism.

Dr. Keller played a small role in helping *Warriors Don't Cry* in becoming a celebrated play. The author recommends you see the play and buy all the civil rights movement books published by this great American author, Dr. Melba Patillo Beals. See Exhibit 1 for other books by Dr. Beals.

Dr. Keller encourages you to learn about all of the Little Rock Nine and read the inspiring books they have written and that have been written about them. The nine civil rights heroes are Thelma Mothershed Wair, Minnijean Brown Trickey, Jefferson Thomas, Terrence Roberts, Carlotta Walls LaNier (*A Mighty Long Way: My Journey to Justice at Little Rock Central High School*), Gloria Ray Karlmark, Ernest Green, Elizabeth Eckford, and Melba Pattillo Beals.

The National Park Service released this statement about the Little Rock Nine when it designated Little Rock High School as a National Historic Site,

"In 1957, nine ordinary teenagers walked out of their homes and stepped up to the front lines in the battle for civil rights for all Americans. The media coined the name 'Little Rock Nine,' to identify the first African-American students to desegregate Little Rock Central High School." Go to www.nps.gov to learn more.

Above: Photo taken at the 1999 Little Rock Nine White House Ceremony. Photo credit: William Jefferson Clinton Presidential Library. The Library circled Dr. Keller's image in the back left as they used facial recognition to locate the photo of the person making the photo request.

Dr. Keller gets involved in politics when he believes he can make a humanitarian-based difference. He took a year off from college to become the International Co-Director of Operation Outrage to help send food and medical supplies to starving children in war-torn Biafra in Southern Nigeria. During that time, Dr. Keller wrote memorialization legislation about that crisis that was unanimously passed in various states.

In that same period, Dr. Keller was the organizing Chairman of a U.S. Congressional Campaign in Maryland whose candidate wanted to save American and Asian lives by seeking a resolution to U.S. involvement in Vietnam. He was tear-gassed at a peaceful rally in Chicago. He successfully wrote, launched, and won a ballot proposition in the State of California. In 2018 Dr. Keller worked on the Democratic gubernatorial campaign in Florida for African-American Andrew Gillum.

Dr. Keller's background includes being a Catholic altar boy and attending a high school seminary.

Dr. Keller spent nearly a decade in the commercial arts, advertising, media, film, TV, public relations, and news industries. During that time, he won a producer's award for special effects in a short-film honoring the Nez Perce Native American Indians called *Legend Days Are Over*.

Keller has four inventions. As a Senior Sales Executive for XEROX Corporation Keller invented the ADT™ accessory to XEROX' most expensive $250,000 device, increasing sales by $98 million per year.

Following that, with funds from successful real estate investments, Dr. Keller invented and successfully launched an FDA regulated isotonic nutraceutical micro-nutrient product that helped patients with HIV-AIDS. Some of Dr. Keller's most precious memories are letters from mothers of sons with HIV-AIDS who said their sons received comfort and benefits from his isotonic-balanced micro-nutrient product. Those proprietary isotonic formulas are available today to the right company or entrepreneur.

Keller invented a mortgage industry product called the insured and warranted automatic valuation model. That accomplishment, combined with his creation of the *Loan Portfolio Triage* analytical tool, resulted in a Fortune 100 company, First American Title Corp, asking him to represent them to the largest banks in Australia.

As part of his PhD dissertation, Dr. Keller's fourth invention was MicroMindfulness™. Studies show that this 30-second technique will reduce heart rate and enhance mood. He demonstrated MicroMindfulness™ at Google headquarters, and one engineer said it cleared his mind, "like emptying the RAM space."

Keller Research Institute, KRI, is a non-profit educational organization that seeks donations to fund humanitarian projects.

One KRI project is a life-saving bicycle accessory, which has a registered trademark, and a patent-pending. It will save lives and reduce serious injuries. KRI seeks assistance in its production and launch.

Another KRI project is a short video for climate deniers. KRI wants to produce a short climate-change YouTube video for climate-change deniers that demonstrates that we live in a sealed environment, similar to a sealed garage with similar risks and dangers. Draft script available.

Dr. Keller is available to support worthy projects and people.

Dr. Keller is available as a consultant.

Dr. Keller is available for interviews and speaking engagements.

DrDavidKingKeller@gmail.com

In Gratitude

To my partner, my wife.

Publisher's Terms and Conditions

Readers and Users of This Book's Content Accept These Publisher's Terms and Conditions As a Pre-condition To Reading or Using This Book or Any Portion Thereof In Any Manner or For Any Reason and Use of This Book or Its Contents In any Manner Is Agreement To a Complete Release of Liability For Any Harm of Any Type Including Reputational Harm. Reviewers may use accredited excerpts. Free rights to use of political cartoons. This book is about education and encouraging dialogue. Changes in future versions of this book will be based on new research and feedback. In order to protect the First Amendment rights and other rights of the author, publisher, and other contributors, the user of any element of this book or portion thereof for any reason (User) accepts these Publisher's Terms and Conditions as a pre-condition of use. These Publisher's Terms and Conditions are not separable from any of the Book's content. User agrees with David King Keller, PhD (Author) and Keller Research Institute (Publisher) that nothing in this Book is intended to, or does, cause harm or damage of any type to anyone, or any group or organization, and User further agrees not to participate in any action making any claim to the contrary (Participant), but if a User becomes a Participant, that Participant / User now agrees to assume all costs incurred by Author or Publisher in defense of any action or claim if same is brought about by and related actions of the Participant/User. Simply possessing this Book or any of its contents does not release the User of any obligations pursuant to these Terms and Conditions herein. The User holds Author and Publisher harmless of any and all loss or damage of any type. User agrees not to share any of the Book's content with anyone prior to that party agreeing to these same Terms and Conditions, and violation of this last-mentioned term makes the User a Participant. User agrees any claimed harm may be satisfactorily resolved by an edit of the current manuscript, which impacts all future releases utilizing that edited manuscript. This book is for educational purposes intended to encourage thoughtful dialogue about the issues reviewed herein. Legally protected parody is included.

Index

2016 election, 16

ACA, 21, 22, 23

Affordable Care Act, 21

African-American, 23

African-Americans, 16

Alexandria Ocasio-Cortez, 23

Ayanna Pressley, 23

Bernie Sanders, 18

Biden, 6, 27

blacks, 11

Clinton, 6, 17

David King Keller, 2, 40

dog whistles, 12, 13

Dr. Melba Patillo Beals, 30

Elizabeth Warren, 18

George Bush, 15

Hillary Clinton, 11, 16

Ilhan Omar, 23

Jason McDaniel, 17

Keller Research Institute, 37, 40

Keller, David King, 40

Little Rock Nine, 34

Martin Luther King's Poor People's Campaign, 33

Medicare, 22

Mexican, 12

millennial, 10

millennials, 10

Millennials, 10

nationalists, 12, 15, 16, 18, 24, 25

Pew Research, 10

Poll
Trump is a racist, 6

President Bill Clinton, 34

Quinnipiac Poll-Trump Racist, 6

racial discontent, 24

racial resentment, 6, 7, 9, 11, 12, 13, 14, 15, 17, 20, 23, 24, 25, 31

racism, 9, 12, 13, 14, 17, 24, 25

Racists, 24

Rashida Tlaib, 23

Republikkkan Party, 21

sexism, 12

Supreme Court, 15

The Squad, 23

Trump, 23

Warriors Don't Cry, 30

Washington Post, 11

white grievance, 6, 7, 8, 11, 24, 25

White House, 34

white nationalists, 6

white supremacists, 12

"Everybody can be great … because anybody can serve.

-	Dr. Martin Luther King

"Until I am welcomed everywhere as an equal simply because I am human, I remain a warrior on a battlefield that I must not leave. I continue to be a warrior who does not **cry** but who instead takes action.

-	Dr. Melba Patillo Beals,
From her book, *Warriors Don't Cry*

"Unconditional love can co-exist with unconditional resistance to racism in all its forms."

-	Dr. David King Keller

www.ingramcontent.com/pod-product-compliance
Lightning Source LLC
Chambersburg PA
CBHW050709250726
48662CB00002B/921